Nelson

Handwriting

Developing Skills

2

BOOK TWO

Anita Warwick

Series editor: John Jackman

 Nelson Thornes

Page	Focus	Extra	Extension	Focus resource	Extension resource
4-5 Flashback	*Flashback*	*Flashback*	*Flashback*	*Flashback*	*Flashback*
6-7 Unit 1 Vikings	practising consistency in size and proportion of letters: rr ll tt dd	copy words ending in ing	copy passage	trace and copy pattern, double consonants and words	copy passage
8-9 Unit 2 Vikings	practising using a diagonal joining line: ship, ment, ness, less	add suffix and copy words	choose words and copy sentences	trace and copy pattern, suffixes and words	choose correct words, complete and copy sentences
10-11 Unit 3 China and India	practising leaving an equal space between letters: ary, ery, cry, dry	copy words ending in ary	copy postcard and fill in missing letters	trace and copy pattern and words ending with ary, ery, cry, dry	choose correct words, complete and copy sentences
12-13 Unit 4 China and India	practising joining to the letter y: ly, ily, ity, ify	add suffix to words, remove e in words ending in e before adding suffix, copy words	choose words and copy sentences	trace and copy pattern and words ending with ily, ity, ify	choose correct words, complete and copy sentences
14-15 Unit 5 Flood	practising using a horizontal joining line: row, now, how, bow	change one letter to show a change of tense and copy words	choose words and copy sentences	trace and copy pattern and words featuring row, now, how and bow	match and copy words in past and present tense
16-17 Unit 6 Flood	practising the size and height of letters: ried, ries, rief	change y to i before adding es or ed, leave y when adding ing, copy words	copy poem	trace and copy pattern and words ending with ried and ries	complete tables adding s, ed and ing to words
18-19 Unit 7 Fireworks	practising joining from the letter i: lig, rig, nig, mig	copy words ending in ight and ite	copy poem	trace and copy pattern, make and copy words ending with ight, write own sentence	complete and copy sentences choosing missing ight or ite word
20-21 Unit 8 Fireworks	practising joining to and from the letter v: live, tive, sive, five	copy words made from explode and act	choose words and copy sentences	trace and copy pattern and words ending with ive and tive, write own sentence	complete and copy sentences choosing a word ending with sive or tive
22-23 Unit 9 Castles	practising consistency in forming and joining letters: ear, are, rew, new	copy homophones	choose words and copy sentences	trace and copy pattern, make and copy words ending with ear and are	practise writing homophones using ee and ea words, write own sentence
24-25 Unit 10 Castles	practising speedwriting: speedily, quickly, swiftly, briskly	use speedwriting to copy 'directional' words	put instructions in correct order and copy in speedwriting	copy sentences to practise speedwriting	copy passage and work out writing speed

Page	Focus	Extra	Extension	Focus resource	Extension resource
26-27 Unit 11 Rubbish and Pollution	practising crossing double tt on completing the word: itt, utt, att, ott	copy two-syllable words containing double consonants	copy poem	trace and copy pattern, copy words containing att and ott	copy poem
28-29 Unit 12 Rubbish and Pollution	practising joining to and from the letter e: rec, red, ved, ves	add s and d to words ending in e, drop e and add ing, copy words	copy poem	trace and copy pattern, copy words ending with f, fe that change to ves in the plural	copy poem
30-31 Unit 13 Snow	practising joining to and from the letter w: owf, owb, owm, owd	copy compound words including the word snow	copy haiku poem	trace and copy pattern and compound words using base words ward and work	copy haiku and cinquain poems
32-33 Unit 14 Snow	practising joining to the letter a from the letter w: wan, was, wav, wax	copy words beginning with wa	copy poem	trace and copy pattern and words containing wa, write own sentence	complete and copy sentences choosing a word containing wa
34-35 Unit 15 Bridges and Fire	practising speedwriting	copy shortened words	copy message using speedwriting and shortened words	write the meaning of a detective's notes	practise speedwriting to write a pizza order
36-37 Unit 16 Bridges	practising printing	copy printed 'rhyming' words	put captions in correct order and copy them	use print to write labels on a street plan	use print to write the names of cities on a map
38-39 Unit 17 Famous Author	practising drafting and editing	write new draft about Roald Dahl	copy corrected draft about Roald Dahl	write a neat copy, with corrected spellings, of the first draft of a story	write a neat copy of the first draft of a story choosing words to replace ones crossed out
40-41 Unit 18 Famous Author	practising speedwriting	copy words and their abbreviations	use shortened words in a list of ingredients for a hot chocolate drink and copy list	writing numerals and number words 11-20	write notes from a newspaper article
42-43 Unit 19 Country Pursuits	practising joining to the letter t: its, lts, tts, uts	choose the correct word its or it's and copy sentences	copy poem	choose words and complete sentences	copy poem
44-45 Unit 20 Country Pursuits	practising printing	draw and print rosettes	design a poster	copy the print alphabet and numerals	copy poster
46-48 Check-up	*Check-up*	*Check-up*	*Check-up*	*Check-up*	*Check-up*

FLASHBACK

OCUS

Copy these patterns into your book.

ococ ococ ococ ococ

Ull Ull Ull Ull

MMM MMM MMM MMM

nene nene nene nene

wrwr wrwr wrwr wrwr

☰Oııllo ☰Oııllo ☰Oııllo ☰Oııllo

4

EXTRA

Copy these words into your book.

lead leading new blew whirly
making caring truck trick chillier
rainiest first firstly nonsense
where's which whichever flex flew

EXTENSION

Copy this poem into your book.

Why is my face
At the front of my head?
Why is my tongue
All pinky-red?

Why do I walk
With my feet on the floor?
Why am I taller
Than I was before?

From **'Why?'** by *Ronald Kay*

Practising consistency in size and proportion of letters.

ki

Viking attack!

FOCUS

A Copy this pattern into your book.

m ШШ ccc m ШШ ccc

B Copy these letters into your book.

rr   rr   rr   rr   rr

U   U   U   U   U

tt   tt   tt   tt   tt

dd   dd   dd   dd   dd

Remember, the letter *t* is not as tall as other letters with an ascender.

EXTRA

Copy these words into your book.

getting   letting

carrying   marrying

spilling   thrilling

Remember to make sure your letters are consistent in size.

EXTENSION

Copy this passage into your book.

The boat pulls up by the bank. It is full of huge men, with long, fair hair underneath iron helmets. With hardly a sound, they spill out of the boat, lifting off their round shields to take with them. They are all carrying axes and swords.

From 'Raiders!' by Lynne Benton

Practising using a diagonal joining line.

I can see Viking ships!

FOCUS

A Copy this pattern into your book.

neni neni neni neni

B Copy these letters into your book.

ship ship ship ship ship
ment ment ment ment ment
ness ness ness ness ness
less less less less less

Remember, a diagonal joining line joins letters together *at* or *near* the top of the next letter, like this:

ship

Adding a suffix to a word makes a new word.
Copy these words into your book.

> dictator + ship = dictatorship
>
> false + hood = falsehood
>
> govern + ment = government

 **XTENSION**

Choose the correct word to finish these sentences. Copy the sentences into your book.

1 King Alfred was determined to overthrow Lord Guthrum, who had established a dictator/dictatorship.

2 In an act of false/falsehood, Alfred put on a dress as a disguise.

3 Alfred defeated the Vikings in 878 and established a just and fair govern/government.

Practising the size and height of letters.

She cried floods of tears.

FOCUS

A Copy this pattern into your book.

ᴙᴧᴧ ᴧᴧᴧ ᴧᴧᴧ ᴧᴧᴧ

B Copy these letters into your book.

ried ried ried ried ried

ries ries ries ries ries

rief rief rief rief rief

 **XTRA**

Copy these words into your book.

cry	cries	cried	crying
dry	dries	dried	drying
try	tries	tried	trying
fry	fries	fried	frying

Remember,
the descender, or tail,
on a letter goes below
the line.

 **XTENSION**

Copy this poem into your book.
Write the title in capital letters.

BOO HOO

Mabel cried as she stood
  by the window,
Mabel cried as she stood
  by the door.
Mabel cried and her tears
  filled three buckets;
Mabel cried as she sat on the floor.

By *Arnold Spilka*

Practising joining from the letter **i**.

ig

Sparklers are little bright lights.

FOCUS

A Copy this pattern into your book.

ig   ig   ig   ig

B Copy these letters into your book.

lig   lig   lig   lig   lig

rig   rig   rig   rig   rig

nig   nig   nig   nig   nig

mig   mig   mig   mig   mig

Remember, when you join from the letter *i* to the letter *g*, go to the top and then back round, like this:

ig

XTRA

Make these words. Copy them into your book.

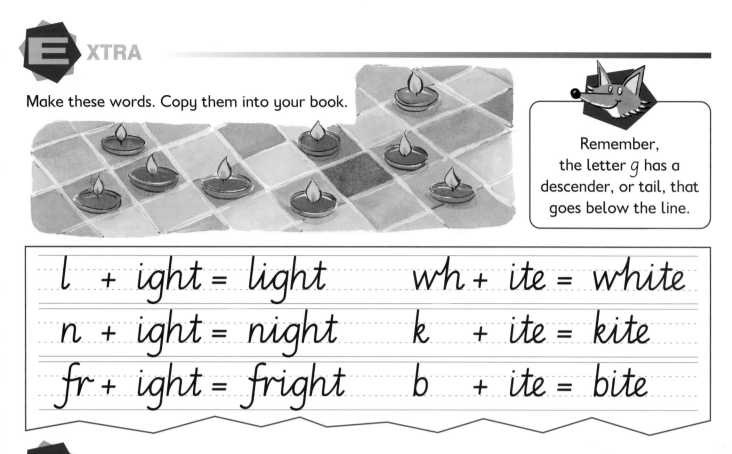

Remember, the letter *g* has a descender, or tail, that goes below the line.

l + ight = light	wh + ite = white
n + ight = night	k + ite = kite
fr + ight = fright	b + ite = bite

EXTENSION

Copy this poem into your book. Write the title in capital letters.

Use your best handwriting when you want to present neat, careful work.

FIREWORKS

They rise like sudden fiery flowers
That burst upon the night,
Then fall to earth in burning showers
Of crimson, blue, and white.

from *'Fireworks'* by *James Reeves*

Practising joining to and from the letter v.

ive

Five rockets were very lively.

FOCUS

A Copy this pattern into your book.

reve reve reve reve

B Copy these letters into your book.

live	*live*	*live*	*live*	*live*
tive	*tive*	*tive*	*tive*	*tive*
sive	*sive*	*sive*	*sive*	*sive*
five	*five*	*five*	*five*	*five*

Remember,
when joining the letter
v to the letter *e*, make
sure you form the *e*
correctly, like this:

ve ✓   *ve* ✗

Copy these words into your book.

explode	act
exploding	acting
explosive	active
explosion	action

Remember, the letter
x is a break letter.
It does not join.

EXTENSION

Choose the correct word to finish these sentences.
Copy the sentences into your book.

1 Guy Fawkes put an explode/explosive charge under the Houses of Parliament.

2 This act/active is remembered as 'The Gunpowder Plot'.

21

Practising consistency in forming and joining letters.

ar

Beware of the bows and arrows!

FOCUS

A Copy this pattern into your book.

crcr crcr crcr crcr

B Copy these letters into your book.

ear ear ear ear ear
are are are are are
new new new new new
new new new new new

Make sure all these letters are the same size and height.

EXTRA

Homophones are words that sound the same but are spelt differently.
Copy these homophones into your book.

bare bear	right rite	threw through
hare hair	might mite	knew new
fare fair	night knight	yew you

EXTENSION

Choose the correct homophone to finish these sentences.
Copy the sentences into your book.

1 Soldiers armed with bows and arrows attacked the castle at night/knight.

2 All the knights in the castle knew/new their own horse.

3 The princess in the castle tower let down her hare/hair.

Practising speedwriting.

Turn right to get to the castle.

FOCUS

A Copy this pattern into your book.

UUUU   UUUU   UUUU   UUUU

B Copy these words in speedwriting into your book.

speedily speedily speedily
quickly quickly quickly
swiftly swiftly swiftly
briskly briskly briskly

You use speedwriting when you need to write something quickly, such as directions. Your handwriting doesn't have to be neat but it must be readable.

EXTRA

A Copy these words in speedwriting into your book.

through beneath
behind across
left right up down

B See how many times you can write the words in one minute.

EXTENSION

Put these instructions in the correct order.
Use speedwriting to copy the instructions into your book.

1 Follow the stairs up to the top of the tower to find two doors.

2 Go through the green door on the right.

3 Bring the drawbridge down to cross the moat.

4 The treasure is behind the throne on the left.

Practising crossing double **tt** on completing the word.

Litter flows along the gutter.

FOCUS

A Copy this pattern into your book.

B Copy these letters into your book.

itt itt itt itt itt

utt utt utt utt utt

att att att att att

ott ott ott ott ott

Cross double *tt* after you have finished joining the letters.

EXTRA

Copy these words into your book.

litter	mutter	rattle
fitter	gutter	battle
bitter	clutter	cattle

Remember to cross your double *tt* after you have finished writing the whole word.

EXTENSION

Copy this poem into your book. Write the title in capital letters.

GRANDAD SAYS

Remember to use your best handwriting when you want to present neat, careful work.

On the pavements, in the streets,
Bags from crisps, wrappers from sweets.
Rubbish rots in roads and gutters.
"What a mess!" Grandad mutters.
"Keep things tidy, keep things clean.
Make the world fit to be seen."

By *Irene Yates*

rec

Protect the environment and recycle!

FOCUS

A Copy this pattern into your book.

ecec ecec ecec ecec

B Copy these letters into your book.

rec rec rec rec rec
red red red red red
ved ved ved ved ved
ves ves ves ves ves

Remember, when joining the letters r or v to e, you need to bring the join *down* to meet the letter e, like this:

re

 **XTRA**

Copy these words into your book.

recycle	recycles	recycled	recycling
save	saves	saved	saving
use	uses	used	using

 **XTENSION**

Copy this poem into your book. Write the title in capital letters.

WE'VE GOT TO START RECYCLING

Take all your old glass bottles
To the bottle bank in town,
So they can use the glass again
By melting it all down.

Don't throw away your drink cans,
Their metal's useful too.
We've got to start recycling.
It's up to me and you!

By *John Foster*

Practising joining to and from the letter **w**.

owf

A snowfall can be fun!

FOCUS

A Copy this pattern into your book.

owow owow owow owow

B Copy these letters into your book.

owf   owf   owf   owf   owf
owb   owb   owb   owb   owb
owm   owm   owm   owm   owm
owd   owd   owd   owd   owd

Remember,
the horizontal join will
help you to keep the
correct space between
your letters.

 **EXTRA**

Copy these compound words into your book.

| snowfall | snowman | snowflake |
| snowball | snowdrift | snowdrop |

 EXTENSION

A haiku is a single-verse poem with three lines.
Lines one and three each contain five syllables
and line two contains seven syllables.
Copy this haiku into your book.
Write the title in capital letters.

Remember to use your
best handwriting when
you want to present
neat, careful work.

HAIKU
Snowman in a field
listening to the raindrops
wishing him farewell

By *Roger McGough*

Practising joining to the letter a from the letter w.

When snow melts, it turns into water.

Focus

A Copy this pattern into your book.

wawa wawa wawa wawa

B Copy these letters into your book.

wan wan wan wan wan

was was was was was

wav wav wav wav wav

wax wax wax wax wax

Don't forget to leave enough space between your letters.

Copy these words into your book.

was	wand	wax
wash	wander	wave
wasp	want	wait

The joining lines help you to leave an equal space between your letters.

EXTENSION

Copy this poem into your book. Write the title in capital letters.

WHEN ALL THE WORLD IS FULL OF SNOW

I never know
just where to go,
when all the world
is full of snow.

I do not want
to make a track,
not even
to the shed and back.

By N. M. Bodecker

Practising speedwriting.

Urgent message!

FOCUS

A Copy this pattern into your book.

cd cd cd cd cd cd cd cd

B Copy these words in speedwriting into your book.

department

ten o'clock

accident and emergency

as soon as possible

Remember, you use speedwriting when you need to write something quickly, such as a note. Your handwriting doesn't have to be neat but it must be readable.

The words below have a shortened form, which is
useful in speedwriting. Copy the words into your book.

Road = Rd

number = no.

we will = we'll

there is = there's

as soon as possible = a.s.a.p.

ten o'clock tonight = 10.00p.m.

accident and emergency = A and E

EXTENSION

Copy this message into your book in speedwriting.
Use the shortened forms from the **Extra** above.

Urgent message

Ten o'clock tonight

There is a fire at the old bridge
on London Road. Send out fire engine
number three as soon as possible.
We will contact the accident and
emergency department to let them know.

Practising printing to make captions.

Aa

We can use print writing for captions.

FOCUS

This is the print alphabet. Copy the letters into your book.

Aa Bb Cc Dd Ee Ff Gg
Hh Ii Jj Kk Ll Mm Nn
Oo Pp Qq Rr Ss Tt Uu
Vv Ww Xx Yy Zz

EXTRA

Copy these printed words into your book.

hop	hand	ridge	kicks
crop	land	fridge	licks
drop	stand	bridge	sticks

EXTENSION

Put these captions in the correct order to match the pictures.
Copy the captions into your book.

Stand on a bridge over a stream.

The stick you see first wins.

Drop the sticks into the water.

Watch from the other side
  of the bridge.

Find two sticks.

Practising drafting and editing.

Roald Dahl wrote famously funny books.

FOCUS

These words have been edited.
Write the corrected words into your book.

tool k	b est	funn y
b o ok	g u est	bunney
loo k	qu e st	runn y

Correcting your writing in the first draft will help you produce a neat and tidy final draft.

This draft has been edited.
Write the new draft into your book.

Roald

R. Dahl was born in 1817/1917 and died in 1990. He wrote the funniest children's books in the world! In 1964 he wrote his best-selling book 'Charlie and the Chocolate Factory'.

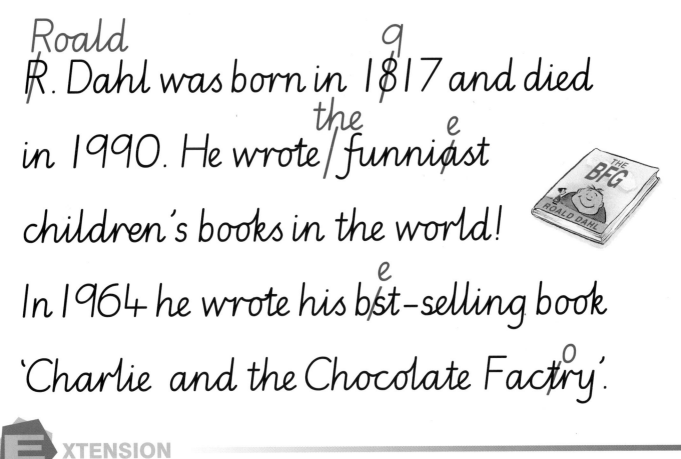

EXTENSION

Use your best handwriting to copy this final draft into your book.

My favourite Roald Dahl book is 'The Twits'. It is about Mr and Mrs Twit and the tricks they play on each other. The worm spaghetti was the best trick and made me laugh!

Practising speedwriting.

Favourite authors

Shorten words to help you write quickly.

FOCUS

A Copy this pattern into your book.

nnn nnn nnn nnn

B Copy these words and numbers into your book.

one two three four five
1   2   3   4   5

six seven eight nine ten
6   7   8   9   10

Remember, you use speedwriting when you need to write something quickly, such as a list. Your handwriting doesn't have to be neat but it must be readable.

SHOPPING LIST
milk
bread
eggs
butter
Tea

TO DO LIST
Tidy my room
walk dog
Do my homework

Homework list
history
maths - uck!
english

EXTRA

The words below have a shortened form, which is useful in speedwriting.
Copy the words into your book.

teaspoon (s)   = tsp   millilitre (s) = ml
tablespoon (s) = tbsp   centilitre (s) = cl
dessertspoon (s) = dsp   litre (s)   = l

EXTENSION

Copy this list of ingredients into your book in speedwriting.
Use the shortened forms from the **Focus** and the **Extra**.

Charlie's Hot Chocolate

three teaspoons of cocoa powder
one hundred and seventy five
    millilitres of warm milk
two marshmallows
four tablespoons of
    whipped cream
one dessertspoon of
    chocolate sprinkles

Practising joining to the letter **t**.

it

It's up to us to protect the countryside.

FOCUS

A Copy this pattern into your book.

uuu   uuu   uuu   uuu

B Copy these letters into your book.

its   its   its   its   its
lts   lts   lts   lts   lts
tts   tts   tts   tts   tts
uts   uts   uts   uts   uts

Remember, the letter *t* is not as tall as other letters with an ascender.

EXTRA

its and **it's** are often confused but
it's = it is and *its = belonging to it.*

Choose the correct word to finish each sentence. Copy the sentences into your book.

1 We saw a bird make *its/it's* nest in the tree.

2 *Its/It's* important to take your litter home with you.

> Remember to use your best handwriting when you want to present neat, careful work.

EXTENSION

Copy this poem into your book. Write the title in capital letters.

WE MUST PROTECT THE COUNTRYSIDE

We must protect the countryside –
The flowers and the trees.
We must protect the animals.
It's up to you and me.

Don't throw litter on the ground.
Please put it in a bin,
And close the gate behind you
To keep the cattle in.

By *John Foster*

Practising printing to make a poster.

T t

Country Fair Today!

FOCUS

A Copy this pattern into your book.

llo||ollo||oll llo||ollo||oll llo||ollo||oll

B Copy the days of the week into your book in print handwriting.

Monday Tuesday Wednesday
Thursday Friday Saturday
Sunday

Remember,
when printing your
letters, do not join them.

Draw three rosettes in your book.
Copy these words in print on to the rosettes.

SPECIAL MENTION
The best-groomed pony

FIRST PRIZE
Clearing all
the jumps

FUNNIEST PRIZE
Knocking down all the
jumps

E XTENSION

Design your own poster for the Country Fair.
Copy these details in print on to the poster.

COUNTRY FAIR
Saturday 11th June
10.00 a.m.
Nelson Manor Gardens
Only 50p
Riding competition and bouncy castle

OCUS

Copy these patterns into your book.

nenu nenu nenu nenu

rur rur rur rur

lili lili lili lili

owow owow owow owow

fofo fofo fofo fofo

llollollollollollolloll llollollollollollolloll llollollollollollolloll

Copy these words into your book.

new knew night knight
act acting active
fright light simplify
correctly mutter clutter
February grew grow
explode explosion
white kite snowball snowflake
government dictatorship falsehood

Use your best handwriting to copy this poem into your book or on to plain paper.

Gravy, gravy, give us gravy
We like gravy with EVERYthing
Gravy with fish
Gravy with cheese
Gravy with sausage
Gravy with peas
Gravy, gravy, give us gravy
We like gravy with EVERYthing.

Gravy, gravy, give us gravy
We like gravy with EVERYthing
Gravy with eggs
Gravy with custard
Gravy with ice-cream
Gravy with mustard
Gravy, gravy, give us gravy
We like gravy with EVERYthing.

(Anonymous)